COME ON ENGLAND

EURO 2004 PREVIEW

p

This is a Parragon Book
First Published in 2004

Parragon, Queen Street House, 4 Queen Street, Bath BA1 1HE, UK

ISBN 1-40542-999-2

Text written by Kevin Connolly
Designed by designsection

Printed in China

CONTENTS

England reached the finals of Euro 2004 without losing a game. But they did it the hard way…

The opening game in Slovakia set the pattern. England went behind when Szilard Nemeth pounced on a rebound. But David Beckham and Michael Owen came to the rescue with two second-half goals. Macedonia were stubborn too. Artem Sakiri gave them a 10th-minute lead with a corner that swirled over David Seaman. Beckham drilled Eriksson's team level. Vanco Trajanov shocked England when he curled a 25-yarder past Seaman. But Steven Gerrard fired a second equaliser from Beckham's header. It was the last game of Seaman's distinguished England career.

By now questions were being asked about England's prospects. They grew louder after Owen and Beckham had earned England an unimpressive 2-0 win in Liechtenstein.

Eriksson gambles

Against Turkey Eriksson started with 17-year-old Wayne Rooney as Owen's strike partner. The teenager's confidence was the spur the team needed. Turkey keeper Rustu Recber was in defiant mood and kept England out until the 72nd minute. Wayne Bridge swung in a cross. Rio Ferdinand nodded down. Rustu saved again. This time, Darius Vassell was there to poke in the rebound. In stoppage time, Kieron Dyer was fouled and Beckham scored from the spot.

Against Slovakia, England went one down. Gerrard inspired a second-half revival and Owen finished the job, netting the penalty on the hour and then heading the winner – his 22nd England goal in his 50th appearance.

Once more, England went behind in Skopje after Georgi Hristov gave Macedonia a 28th-minute lead. Once more, Eriksson changed tack, sending on Heskey to support Owen and Rooney for the second half. The move paid dividends, as Heskey set up Rooney for the equaliser. Skipper Beckham hit the winner from the spot after John Terry was fouled.

Owen and Rooney scored early in the second half to see off Liechtenstein at Old Trafford.

The 'band of brothers' celebrate after their 0-0 draw with Turkey in Istanbul.

That set up a grand finale in Istanbul in which England needed only a draw to advance as group winners. A superb performance by referee Collina and some intelligent defending by England was enough to secure qualification. The whole party danced a jig of celebration at the final whistle. 'We were like a band of brothers,' said John Terry.

England had come a long way since those opening moments against Slovakia.

ENGLAND'S RESULTS

EURO 2004 QUALIFYING ROUND – GROUP SEVEN

Slovakia 1-2 England (Beckham, Owen)
England 2-2 Macedonia (Beckham, Gerrard)
Liechtenstein 0-2 England (Owen, Beckham)
England 2-0 Turkey (Vassell, Beckham, pen)
England 2-1 Slovakia (Owen 2, 1 pen)
Macedonia 1-2 England (Rooney, Beckham, pen)
England 2-0 Liechtenstein (Owen, Rooney)
Turkey 0-0 England

EURO 2004: THE CONTENDERS

EURO 2004 TIMETABLE

Opening match: 12 June
Group games: 12-23 June
Quarter-finals: 26 and 27 June
Semi-finals: 30 June and 1 July
Final: 4 July

Holders France, hosts Portugal and Euro 2000 runners-up Italy head England's list of rivals as the European Championship finals build to a crescendo. Germany, the surprise 2002 World Cup finalists, will fancy their chances too, and the surprise package could be the Czech Republic, who beat Holland to qualify from Group Three.

The French are determined to lay the bitter memories of the 2002 World Cup to rest. They arrived as favourites, crashed to defeat against Senegal, then went home after losing to Denmark. France's Far East disaster cost coach Roger Lemerre his job. But France boast the best record of all the qualifiers. They were the only team to win all eight games, and scored 29 goals in the process. The core of France's Euro 2000 team remains – Lilian Thuram and Bixente Lizarazu in defence, Patrick Vieira and Zinedine Zidane in midfield, supported by Robert Pires, Thierry Henry and David Trezeguet up front. Coach Jacques Santini is praying that they carry their qualifying form to Portugal.

Portugal's solid backbone

The hosts will never have a better chance of improving on their semi-final finish in 1984, when they lost a memorable contest to France in Marseille. Luis Figo is their star, and their talisman Rui Costa will pull the strings in midfield. A bevy of players from UEFA Cup holders Porto provide a solid backbone for the hosts. Home support will be an added advantage. Portugal also have World Cup disappointment to put behind them.

So do Italy, the Golden Goal losers to France four years

ago. Alessandro Nesta and Fabio Cannavaro present a formidable barrier in front of the world's most expensive goalkeeper, Gigi Buffon. The mercurial Francesco Totti will inspire them. Veteran coach Giovanni Trapattoni can choose from a wealth of attacking riches – Christian Vieri, Alessandro del Piero, Pippo Inzaghi and Marco Di Vaio.

Germany, winners in 1996, were unbeaten in heading Group Five. Michael Ballack is Europe's most potent attacking midfielder. His Bayern Munich colleague Oliver Kahn remains one of the continent's top keepers. The emergence of Stuttgart striker Kevin Kuranyi has given the Germans a cutting edge they've lacked.

The Czechs, Euro '96 runners-up, are the dark horses. Karel Poborsky, their star in England, continues to defy the years. Playmaker Tomas Rosicky and the dashing Pavel Nedved can unlock the best defences. For a more direct option, they can seek the head of 6 foot 7 inch striker Jan Koller.

But, as Sven-Goran Eriksson says: 'England shouldn't be afraid of any team. In the important games, this team has stood up many times and been very, very strong. I can't say we will win Euro 2004, but we're good enough to win it…'

Striker Thierry Henry's form could be the key to French success in Portugal.

David Beckham

Midfielder ◆ Age 28

England's National Icon

David Beckham is a national icon and a worldwide brand name. No other professional sportsman has the commercial appeal of the Real Madrid midfielder. Beckham's popularity in the Far East – and the thousands of shirts his name sells – was undoubtedly a factor in Madrid's move for the England captain. He was mobbed on their tour to Japan, feted in Hong Kong and even used to spearhead an advertising campaign to sell motor oil in Vietnam!

His marriage to Victoria (aka Posh Spice) has made him an international celebrity. He is forever in the media spotlight. England rugby star Jonny Wilkinson said: 'I'm glad I've got my privacy. I don't know where David gets his spare moments from. His discipline and self-control are something else.'

Amidst all the hype, it's easy to forget what first made Beckham famous. He is one of England's few world-class players of the last generation. A superstar, who won the European Cup and every prize in the English game with Manchester United, before his move to the Bernabeu.

Beckham is the supreme dead ball expert in European football: a deadly free-kick exponent, and, until that night in Istanbul, a faultless penalty-taker. His ability to whip in accurate crosses under close marking created a host of goals

Beckham shows his commitment to England's cause duirng the home victory over Liechtenstein.

for United. He now plays in a more central role for Madrid.

He believes he has already improved through playing with Real's 'galacticos'. He said: 'When you play with great players, you can only learn from them. Even in training, there are things you can take from the likes of Zinedine Zidane, Luis Figo, Ronaldo, Roberto Carlos and Raul.'

FACT FILE

Club: Real Madrid
Born: Leytonstone, 2 May 1975
England caps: 65 (62 starts, 3 as sub)
England goals: 13
Best moment for England: Scoring the penalty winner against Argentina in the 2002 World Cup finals
Worst moment for England: Being sent off against Argentina in the 1998 World Cup finals

Beckham viewed the move to Madrid as his latest challenge in a career packed with them.

'Whenever I've been faced with a challenge I've always reacted in the right way.'

Indeed, his England progress shows how he has changed public perceptions. He was pilloried after his red card against Argentina in Saint-Etienne, and blamed for England's World Cup exit. He suffered the abuse, stayed silent and concentrated on winning over the fans with his performances. In November 2000, caretaker boss Peter Taylor made him captain for the friendly in Italy. Eriksson confirmed that decision. Beckham has matured in the role, off the pitch as well as on it.

Proud to play for England

It was Beckham who guaranteed England an automatic place in the 2002 World Cup finals with a stoppage time free-kick goal against Greece in their final qualifier. By then, he was a national hero. When he was injured by a challenge from Deportivo's Aldo Duscher in a Champions League game, Beckham's chances of making the World Cup finals filled the front pages. Beckham wasn't fully fit in Japan. But he took revenge on Argentina, scoring the only goal from the spot as England beat their old rivals 1-0 in Sapporo.

He netted five goals in England's run to Euro 2004, including the equaliser in the opening game in Slovakia and the penalty winner in Macedonia. And he showed his onfield composure in Istanbul – despite Alpay's taunts – after slipping backwards and ballooning that spot kick over the bar.

There is a confidence about Beckham now, away from the field, a quality that helped him make the switch to Madrid after 12 years with United. He has become the public face of the England team, the media-friendly interviewee before every big game. He is the intermediary between the squad and Eriksson, who trusts him implicitly. It was Beckham who emerged as a peacemaker when the players threatened strike action over Rio Ferdinand's exclusion before the game in Turkey, even if it meant arguing with his best friend and ex-United colleague Gary Neville.

Supporters realise that playing for England matters to Beckham. He has always been willing to play in friendlies. He has always been quick to praise colleagues. He's also helped build a camaraderie that was reflected in the celebrations after the draw in Istanbul. He said: 'The huddle we had at the end to celebrate wasn't something we'd planned. There was the relief of getting through after the week we'd had. And everyone came together because of the bond there is in the squad.'

Michael Owen

Striker ◆ Age 24

The Main Man for England

It was a June night at Middlesbrough. England trailed 1-0 at the interval to Slovakia in the Euro 2004 qualifier. It was Michael Owen's 50th appearance for his country. He was skipper while David Beckham was suspended. He led by example in the second half. First the Liverpool striker was sandwiched by two Slovak defenders. He sprang up to score the penalty for England's equaliser. Then he rose to meet club colleague Steven Gerrard's centre and head the winner.

England coach Sven-Goran Eriksson chided the media afterwards. 'You don't appreciate Michael Owen. You're very spoiled to have him in this country.' He added: 'I'm happy for Michael. It was a good way to show how to be a captain and a good way to celebrate his 50th cap.' Owen preferred to give credit to Eriksson for his half-time team talk. He said: 'We didn't start too well. Eriksson sat us down at the break and calmed us down. His talk really settled us.'

The statistics back up Eriksson about Owen's importance to England. Since Alan Shearer retired in 2000, England have not won any of the six games when Owen has been unavailable. He has netted 13 times in 18 competitive matches for Eriksson. He joint top-scored with five goals (along with David Beckham) in England's Euro 2004 qualifying campaign. He grabbed the winner in Slovakia in the opening game. His goal against Liechtenstein at Old Trafford took him level with Geoff Hurst on 24 for England.

> **'He's already had a great career for England and it's going to get better… His mental strength sets him apart. He never lets his head drop.'** Steven Gerrard on Michael Owen

Owen has been at the top for so long, it's hard to believe that he's only 24. He made his debut, against Chile, at 18 years and two months. He was still 18 when he scored that memorable goal against Argentina in the 1998 World Cup finals. He was the youngest Englishman to gain 50 caps. He was voted PFA Young Player of the Year and BBC Sports Personality of the Year in 1998. He was named European Player of the Year in 2001. He scored twice as Liverpool beat

Opposite: Michael Owen heads England's first goal in the home game with Liechtenstein at Old Trafford.

FACT FILE

Club: Liverpool
Born: Chester, 14 December 1979
England caps: 53 (43 starts, 10 as sub)
England goals: 24
Best moment for England: Scoring a World Cup qualifying hat-trick in the 5-1 win over Germany in Munich in September 2001
Worst moment for England: Being substituted in all three of England's games at Euro 2000

Arsenal 2-1 in the FA Cup final that year and helped his club complete a treble, with the UEFA Cup and the League Cup.

On 1 September 2001, he gave his finest performance for England, striking a hat-trick as Eriksson's team beat Germany 5-1 in Munich to claim pole position in their World Cup qualifiers. He shot England ahead in the 2002 World Cup quarter-final against Brazil. Although they lost the match, Owen had proved himself again at the highest level.

A gruelling exercise programme has overcome the persistent hamstring problems that sidelined him in his early days. He has worked hard to improve on his left side. And his record of headed goals belies his small stature. Owen looks a good bet to beat Bobby Charlton's record of 49 goals for England.

First he has business at Euro 2004 and some memories to put behind him. Owen started all three games at Euro 2000 when England failed to reach the last eight. He was subbed in each of them, despite scoring against Romania.

Then he was acting as a foil for Shearer. Now – whether he is joined by Wayne Rooney, Emile Heskey, or both – Owen is England's main man. As Eriksson says: 'Everyone in world football knows Michael Owen. Every defender has the greatest respect for him.'

Wayne Rooney

Striker ◆ Age 18

Teenage Prodigy

On 11 October 2003 at the Fenerbahce stadium in Istanbul, Wayne Rooney wore a grin as wide as the Bosporus as England celebrated the draw with Turkey that took them to Euro 2004. It was an important night for England's prodigy; a night when he answered questions about his temperament under fire.

The debate had raged as Sven-Goran Eriksson considered how to replace the injured Michael Owen. Rooney should play, said his supporters. He had proved his worth. The doubters questioned the Everton youngster's attitude. He had collected five Premiership yellow cards in less than two months. He had been involved in an incident at Tottenham the previous weekend. Could Eriksson afford to gamble on him in the cauldron of Istanbul?

The England coach put his trust in Rooney. For more than an hour he ran the Turkish defence all over the pitch. He never reacted, however hard his markers tackled. It was another triumph for Rooney, another chapter in a tale that reads like a *Roy of the Rovers* comic strip.

Flashback nearly a year. The date was 19 October 2002. The place Goodison Park. Rooney was still five days short of his 17th birthday. Everton manager David Moyes had eased him into the big time, often as a late substitute. Rooney

FACT FILE

Club: Everton
Born: Liverpool, 24 October 1985
England caps: 9 (6 starts, 3 as sub)
England goals: 3
Best moment for England: Becoming England's youngest-ever scorer when he netted in the Euro 2004 qualifier in Macedonia
Worst moment for England: Being substituted in the Euro 2004 qualifier v Slovakia

stepped off the bench. The score was 1-1 against champions Arsenal. They had not lost a domestic match since December 2001. Time was running out. Rooney pulled the ball out of the air. Arsenal's defenders backed off. The teenager took a pace or two, looked up and from more than 20 yards shot past David Seaman. It was Rooney's first Premiership goal. He had wrecked Arsenal's record. A star was born.

The Rooney bandwagon gathers speed

Two years earlier, he had played for England Under-15s. Now, hardened critics called for him to leap into Sven-Goran Eriksson's senior team. Rooney had vision, skill and the strength to hold off much older opponents. At 17 years, 111 days, he made his England debut, as a substitute in a 3-1 defeat by Australia. He was the youngest debutant in England's history. Less than two months later, Rooney took another step up. On 2 April, England met Turkey in a top-of-the-table Euro 2004 qualifier.

Rooney's moment came in a practice match. Eriksson watched as he broke through one-on-one with Leeds keeper Paul Robinson. The Everton youngster chipped the ball into the top corner of the net with such ease that the other players broke into applause.

Rooney started against the Turks. His enthusiasm galvanised his colleagues. England battled to a 2-0 win against their biggest rivals in Group Seven. Rooney looked like an international veteran. Three minutes before half-time, he sped past two defenders, fed a delicate angled pass into Michael Owen's path. Turkey keeper Rustu Recber saved at Owen's feet. But Rooney had shown his class.

Fast forward to Rooney's sixth cap. On 6 September 2003

'He only knew he was playing at four o'clock. He just said: "OK". It was a very good reaction. He's a great talent and now we know he's ready for the big matches.'

Sven-Goran Eriksson on telling Rooney he was playing against Turkey

Rooney's first start for England saw him run the Turkish defence ragged as his skills lit up the Stadium of Light.

England were 1-0 down at half-time in another qualifier in Macedonia. Eriksson had switched Rooney from his forward role to play behind Owen and sub Emile Heskey. Heskey nodded down David Beckham's pass. Rooney shot low from the edge of the box. England were level. More history in the making. Rooney had beaten Owen's record as England's youngest scorer. He was 17 years and 317 days old.

England won 2-1 through Beckham's penalty and the skipper led the applause for Rooney. Beckham said: 'Wayne is a strong player, a strong character and he has a strong club and family behind him.' Eriksson said: 'I asked Wayne how many times he'd played in the "hole". He said that he'd done it so I told him to go out and do it again.'

Rooney scored again in the same role, four days later against Liechtenstein. Eriksson enthused: 'He's doing very well in that position. He's clever, he plays people in – and he scores goals.'

He's still only 18. His best years are way ahead. That night in Istanbul, he showed that he's added composure to his other gifts. They are frightening thoughts for England's rivals.

Gary Neville

Defender ◆ Age 29

Well Respected Leader

Gary and Phil Neville are the first brothers to play together for England since Bobby and Jack Charlton in the 1960s. Both have points to prove at Euro 2004 after previous disappointments at international finals.

Gary was suspended for the Euro '96 semi-final, which England lost to Germany on penalties. He played in the England side that lost to Argentina on spot kicks in France '98. He started all three games in the Euro 2000 finals when England went home early after the group games. Then he had to sit out the 2002 World Cup after breaking his foot playing for Manchester United against Bayer Leverkusen in the Champions League semi-finals.

Gary has made the right back position his own, for club and country. Former United and England coach Steve McClaren said: 'He brings character and enthusiasm to a team. He's a very reliable defender, aggressive, good positionally and he has a great understanding with David Beckham on the right.'

England's most solid performer

Gary is an organiser, on and off the pitch. McClaren added: 'From the first day that I arrived at Old Trafford, I realised that Gary was one of the most important people in the dressing room. He brings others together. He's a leader and well respected. Other players feel they can turn to him with a problem. It was typical of Gary that he helped his brother through a difficult time after Euro 2000.'

Sometimes, those leadership qualities can land Gary in hot water – like before England's final 2004 qualifier in Istanbul. He was widely seen as the players' 'shop steward' as they threatened to boycott the match in support of the excluded Rio Ferdinand. But, as usual, he turned out to be one of England's most solid performers.

FACT FILE

Club: Manchester United
Born: Bury, 18 February 1975
England caps: 60 (55 starts, 5 as sub)
England goals: 0

Best moment for England: His outstanding defensive performance in England's famous 5-1 World Cup qualifier victory over Germany in Munich in September 2001

Phil Neville

Defender ◆ Age 27

Determination to Succeed

Younger brother Phil missed selection for England's 1998 and 2002 World Cup squads. He played at Euro 2000 but was made a scapegoat after conceding the late penalty against Romania that sealed England's elimination.

If Gary is a specialist, Phil has made a career out of his versatility. It's no surprise that he was a promising young Lancashire cricketer before he joined United. He has won a host of club medals and international caps though rarely a first choice in either. That shows his tenacity, the determination to succeed which overcame the criticism that dogged him after Euro 2000.

He has played for England at right-back, left-back and as a defensive midfielder. He came on as a substitute to anchor midfield in the Euro 2004 qualifying wins over Macedonia and Liechtenstein.

Handy deputy

That may be the role that both Sven-Goran Eriksson and Sir Alex Ferguson believe he fills best. He can slot in for Nicky Butt at the base of England's midfield diamond. He has proved a more than handy deputy for Butt and Roy Keane at United too.

Ask Arsenal. In Keane's absence, he tore through their midfield in the top-of-the-table clash at Old Trafford in 2002-03. He stopped the Gunners playing. United won 2-0 – and rediscovered the momentum that brought them another Premiership title. Phil even scored the only goal in United's 1-0 Champions League win at Rangers this season.

FACT FILE

Club: Manchester United
Born: Bury, 21 January 1977
England caps: 44 (29 starts, 15 as sub)
England goals: 0

Best moment for England: Captaining his country during England's friendly against Serbia and Montenegro at Leicester in June 2003. England won the match 2-1 with goals from Gerrard and Joe Cole

Sol Campbell

Defender ◆ Age 29

The Rock at England's Core

Sol Campbell has towered at the heart of England's defence for years. He made his name in the 1998 World Cup finals and he's never looked back. Sven-Goran Eriksson says: 'Sol is massively experienced.'

The Arsenal centre-back has all the attributes of a top-class defender – strength, aerial power, firm tackling and speed in recovery. But Campbell offers more than that. As Arsenal manager Arsène Wenger says, he has the mental strength to battle through the toughest situations.

None came tougher than Campbell's move from Tottenham to arch rivals Arsenal in the summer of 2001. He was ambitious – and chose to leave when his contract expired. He could have chosen the easy option, a move abroad. Instead, he joined Arsenal, knowing that the Spurs fans would turn on him with a vengeance. And they did. He was heaped with abuse when he returned to White Hart Lane with Arsenal. Campbell kept a dignified silence, won a 'double' with the Gunners, and stepped up to the Champions League. As Eriksson noted: 'He emerged as a true leader after his move to Arsenal.'

Getting the result

It was the same early in 2003-04 when Campbell ran into disciplinary problems with the FA. It was even rumoured that he might stop playing for England. Eriksson urged him to carry on. Campbell responded with a typical performance in the Euro 2004 qualifier in Skopje, shrugging off a misjudgement that contributed to Macedonia's goal, to hold England's back-line together. Such occasions bring out the best in Campbell.

So did that dramatic night in Istanbul. Campbell and John Terry were immense as England held off Turkey's desperate attacks to advance as group winners. Eriksson said: 'Sol and John dealt with all the crosses that came in. Turkey put on strikers who were taller, taller and taller, but it made no difference.' Campbell said: 'The main thing was that we dug in and got the result.' That comment could sum up his career. As Eriksson says: 'We feel more calm when Sol plays. Just his presence is important for us.'

FACT FILE

Club: Arsenal
Born: Newham, 18 September 1974
England caps: 56 (53 starts, 3 as sub)
England goals: 1

Best moment for England: Becoming England's youngest captain since Bobby Moore when he skippered the team in the King Hassan II Tournament match against Belgium in May 1998 in Morocco

Nicky Butt

Midfielder ◆ Age 29

In the Thick of the Action

Nicky Butt has become a key man for England. Butt is the hard-tackling defensive screen at the base of Sven-Goran Eriksson's midfield diamond. It's a job that suits his unselfish but competitive temperament. He made the role his own during the 2002 World Cup finals and filled it to perfection in both Euro 2004 qualifiers against Turkey.

Butt made his England reputation in Japan. Eriksson turned to the United midfielder after Liverpool playmaker Gerrard was ruled out of the World Cup finals with a groin injury. Butt himself had been short of match practice because of a knee problem. He missed the opening 1-1 draw against Sweden – then made a triumphant entry against Argentina.

He disrupted the Argentine midfield by clamping down on his Old Trafford colleague Juan Sebastian Veron. Eriksson said: 'Nicky's performance against Argentina was a very positive surprise. He was outstanding. You'd never have known he'd been away from the action for so long.'

Butt even earned praise from the legendary Pele, despite England's quarter-final defeat by Brazil. Eriksson said: 'He was our star of the tournament, fantastic. He did magnificently.'

Spiky trademark

Those spiky displays became Butt's trademark. He missed the Euro 2004 qualifier in Liechtenstein because of an ankle injury but returned four days later to throw a spanner in Turkey's midfield works as England won 2-0 at Sunderland. He did the same in the 0-0 draw in Istanbul.

Eriksson said: 'Nicky is very important for us. He's a clever player. He takes up very good positions and plays simple balls which is important as a "sitting" midfield player.'

Former England boss Terry Venables rates Butt in the same class as former France anchor Didier Deschamps, who captained his side to World Cup glory in 1998 and Golden Goal victory at Euro 2000. He said: 'Butt understands there's no more valuable job for the team than anchoring the midfield. Think of those who've performed the role in the past: Dunga for Brazil in 1994, Deschamps for France, Gilberto Silva for Brazil in 2002. These are players always in the thick of the action.'

FACT FILE

Club: Manchester United
Born: Manchester, 21 January 1975
England caps: 31 (21 starts, 10 as sub)
England goals: 0

Best moment for England: Being hailed by Sven-Goran Eriksson (and Brazilian legend Pele) as England's best player of the 2002 World Cup finals despite starting the tournament lacking match practice

Ashley Cole

Defender • Age 23

Rare Creature

Ashley Cole's England debut against Albania in March 2001 capped a remarkable rise for the young left-back. Cole is that rare creature of recent times: an Englishman who has advanced through the Arsenal youth ranks to become a Premiership regular.

Cole's future hung in the balance at the start of the 2000-01 season. He had impressed throughout a three-month loan at first division Crystal Palace. There was talk of the move becoming permanent. Then Arsenal's Brazilian left-back Silvinho was injured – and Cole seized his chance.

His emergence coincided with Sven-Goran Eriksson's arrival as England coach. Eriksson included Cole in his first squad, against Spain. A month later, he gambled on the Gunners' youngster in the World Cup qualifier in Tirana. England won 3-1. Cole has been Eriksson's first choice ever since, despite the persistent challenge of Wayne Bridge. His consistency allowed Arsenal to let Silvinho move on to Spain.

A veteran at 23

At 23 Cole is a veteran of the Champions League and the 2002 World Cup finals. As Eriksson said: 'Sometimes we forget that, when I came to England, Ashley was not even a regular at Arsenal.'

Cole has been criticised for lack of defensive discipline. It's no accident that Arsenal's Champions League opponents always try to play balls in behind him. But he has pace – especially in speed of recovery – and a sturdy tackle to add to

his attacking qualities. He has proved that he can mark tight on famous opponents, most notably when he shut Argentina's Ariel Ortega out of the game in the 2002 World Cup finals.

He gave one of his best performances when England drew 0-0 in Turkey to qualify automatically for Euro 2004. That night brought triumph for England and relief for Cole. He admitted: 'I hadn't been on top of my game and that was something I wanted to put right. There was no bigger stage on which to show that I'd resumed normal service.'

FACT FILE

Club: Arsenal
Born: Stepney, 20 December 1980
England caps: 23 (23 starts)
England goals: 0

Best moment for England: Marking playmaker Ariel Ortega out of the game as England beat Argentina 1-0 in the 2002 World Cup finals group stage match in Sapporo, effectively nullifying their attacking flair

Rio Ferdinand

Defender ◆ Age 25

Eager to Prove Himself

Rio Ferdinand's playing future hung in the balance earlier this season. He was excluded by the FA from selection for England's final qualifier in Turkey after failing to take a drugs test. Ferdinand said he 'forgot'. But his memory lapse led to a lengthy investigation and an FA charge for misconduct. It's unlikely that Ferdinand will ever forget a drugs test again. He says he was 'devastated' by the repercussions.

It was Sven-Goran Eriksson who made Ferdinand an England regular, after Kevin Keegan had left him behind for Euro 2000. By then, Europe's elite – led by Real Madrid – were already scouting the cultured West Ham defender. Leeds beat them all, signing him for £18 million in November 2000. Ferdinand skippered them in a Champions League semi-final in his first season.

World Cup triumph

A year later, he captivated a multi-national audience as England reached the 2002 World Cup quarter-finals. Ferdinand pushed and pulled his defence around, jockeying forwards away from danger, winning the ball with clever anticipation and using it shrewdly. His form even drew comparisons with another West Ham and England defender, the legendary Bobby Moore.

Chelsea striker Jimmy Floyd Hasselbaink summed up Ferdinand's quality. 'You barely notice him. He hardly touches you. But he still keeps you out.'

Ferdinand's World Cup displays also clinched a £30 million transfer from Leeds to Manchester United. He admits he wasn't happy with his form in his first year at Old Trafford, even though United won the Premiership. Then he made a nightmare start to the 2003-04 season, missing England's win in Macedonia because of a kidney infection. The drugs test controversy followed.

But Eriksson believes in Ferdinand. He said: 'Rio is an excellent player, one of the best defenders in the world.'

FACT FILE

Club: Manchester United
Born: Peckham, 7 November 1978
England caps: 31
England goals: 1

Best moment for England: Being compared with England's 1966 World Cup-winning captain Bobby Moore after his displays in England's World Cup run in the 2002 finals in Japan and Korea

Emile Heskey

Striker • Age 26

Unselfish Striker

Emile Heskey is a gentle giant. Slow to anger, slow to throw his weight about. He emerged at Leicester as a youngster of formidable physique, pace and power. The Leicester supporters nicknamed him 'Bruno' after the heavyweight champion boxer. But Heskey has never quite translated his attributes into the goals that his admirers anticipated. Critics often question his scoring record, for club and country. But there are few more unselfish strikers.

Working for the team

He accepts without fuss the responsibility of acting as a lone target man, playing out of position on the left, or stepping off the bench as a tactical sub. He made vital contributions as England's Euro 2004 qualifying campaign reached its climax. His arrival as a second-half sub turned the game in Macedonia after England trailed 1-0 at the interval.

It was Heskey who met David Beckham's pass with a cushion header for Wayne Rooney to equalise and become England's youngest-ever scorer. It was Heskey who shouldered the target-man burden in Istanbul, always making himself available for the 'out' ball and winning a series of free kicks with his determination.

Heskey shrugs off the debate about his effectiveness. He said: 'The important thing is that I keep the manager happy, whether it's Sven-Goran Eriksson, or Gérard Houllier at Liverpool.'

Both have kept faith with Heskey. His colleagues appreciate him too. England centre-back John Terry said: 'Emile is a

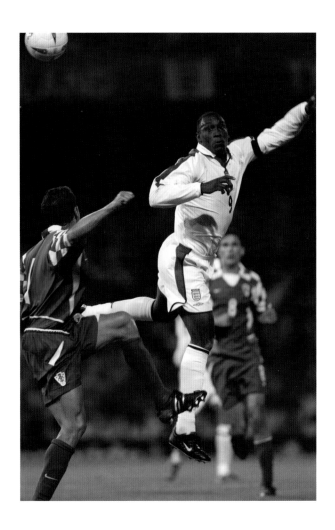

nightmare for defenders to mark. He's a right handful. We get so many free kicks from balls played up to him.'

Michael Owen said: 'Emile is always a threat and he works so hard, tracking back all the time. If I had to keep doing that, I don't think I'd have the legs to make the forward runs. His work helps the whole team, not only me.'

FACT FILE

Club: Liverpool
Born: Leicester, 11 January 1978
England caps: 38 (26 starts, 12 as sub)
England goals: 5

Best moment for England: Scoring the last goal in England's 5-1 demolition of Germany in a World Cup qualifying match in Munich in September 2001 – the third Liverpool player to score that night

Frank Lampard

The Complete Midfield Player

The Chelsea star says club boss Claudio Ranieri deserves the credit for turning him into the complete midfield player. But it's only in the past year that he has finally established his England credentials. He has become a regular in Eriksson's squads and scored his first England goal with a 30-yard strike against Croatia in August.

Lampard made his name at West Ham with attacking flair. But Ranieri has made him recognise his other duties. Lampard said: 'For two years, he's kept on at me about defensive duties and I'm a lot more aware of them than when I was a West Ham player. It's made my whole game stronger.'

Good character

Lampard has his sights set on Euro 2004. He said: 'I've been knocking on the door and I feel a lot more confident about being an England player now. The goal against Croatia gave me confidence and hopefully I can start on a more regular basis. But my club form has to be good. That's a big challenge with all the players who've been brought in.

Ranieri believes Lampard has earned the chance. He said: 'Frank deserves a run in the England side. He can defend, attack, play long or short passes. He can run and tackle and he has a good character.'

FACT FILE

Club: Chelsea
Born: Romford, 20 June 1978
England caps: 16 (8 starts, 8 as sub)
England goals: 1

Best moment for England: Scoring his first England goal – a magnificent 30-yarder – after coming on as a substitute in England's 3-1 friendly win over Croatia at Portman Road in August 2003

There's Only One Steven Gerrard

Steven Gerrard took over the position on the left of England's diamond during the Euro 2004 qualifiers and made it his own. He was outstanding as England curbed Turkey's aggression in Istanbul. It was Gerrard's surge into the box that won England their penalty.

Special player

No other Englishman can match his range of passing, or his understanding with Michael Owen, marked by the early through ball to release the striker's pace. Gerrard has the nous to dictate the tempo too. Add massive energy, a raking tackle and a stinging shot and you have a special player.

If only he weren't so injury-prone. He has played little more than 20 games for his country since 2000. He missed the 2002 World Cup finals after breaking down in Liverpool's last match of the season and needed an operation to cure his groin problem. Yet his injury problems have made him even more determined to succeed for England. He remembers his goal against Germany. 'It was a great feeling. When you've experienced an occasion like that, it makes you even hungrier to get back there.'

Euro 2004 would be the ideal stage. He fancies England's chances. He says: 'I hope we'll be one of the favourites. We've proved that we can mix it with the best. I don't see why we can't win the tournament.'

FACT FILE

Club: Liverpool
Born: Liverpool, 30 May 1980
England caps: 21 (20 starts, 1 as sub)
England goals: 3

Best moment for England: Scoring that magnificent goal on the stroke of half-time to put England ahead in their 5-1 World Cup qualifying win over Germany in Munich in 2001

David James

Goalkeeper ◆ Age 33

James to the Rescue

A match-winning save against Turkey ignited David James's England career after years of waiting in the wings. England led 1-0 with time running out in the Euro 2004 qualifier. Turkey striker Nihat Kahveci headed goalwards. An equaliser looked odds-on, until James tipped the ball to safety. David Beckham added a stoppage-time penalty. England's 2-0 win put them top of Group Seven and established an important psychological advantage over their closest rivals.

England great Ray Clemence, Sven-Goran Eriksson's goalkeeping coach, said: 'The difference between good and great goalkeepers is that the great ones can make saves that influence games. David's save influenced the game without a doubt. It would have been 1-1 if not for that.'

Calamity no more

James has become England's undisputed number 1. He enhanced his reputation with a brilliant display in the 3-1 friendly win over Croatia and ended his Euro 2004 qualifying campaign with a clean sheet against Turkey in Istanbul. Such heights seemed far away during James's early days. He acquired the unwanted nickname of 'Calamity' after errors in high-profile matches while he was at Liverpool in the mid-1990s.

He made his England debut against Mexico in 1997, then had to wait three years for his next cap. For years, he was third choice behind Seaman and Nigel Martyn. And an England call in August 2001 – soon after his move from

Aston Villa to West Ham – ended in disaster. He'd been on the pitch for nine minutes against Holland when he collided with colleague Martin Keown – and he was sidelined for four months with a knee injury.

In 2002-03, he was one of the few players to shine as West Ham were relegated. He admits he feared the drop to Division One might affect his England chances. But Eriksson kept faith. The England coach turned to James to succeed Seaman after the 2-2 draw with Macedonia in the Euro 2004 qualifier at Southampton. He stayed in for the qualifiers against Liechtenstein and Turkey.

James said after the 2002 World Cup finals: 'I enjoyed it, but I didn't play. So my aim is to be in the squad for the Euro 2004 qualifiers, go to the finals in Portugal and do well.'

Now his ambition is within his grasp.

FACT FILE

Club: West Ham United
Born: Welwyn Garden City, 1 August 1970
England caps: 21 (15 starts, 6 as sub)

Best moment for England: Keeping a clean sheet for England against Turkey in Istanbul to cap a confident performance and ensure that England qualified automatically for Euro 2004

Paul Scholes

Midfielder ◆ Age 29

In Search of Goals

Paul Scholes is in search of goals. For years, the Manchester United star was England's most effective support act, arriving unmarked in the box to score important goals. But the 0-0 draw in Istanbul stretched his run without an England goal to more than two years. His last had come in a 2-0 win over Greece in Athens in the World Cup qualifier in June 2001.

England's counter-attacking tactics under Sven-Goran Eriksson have hardly suited the United midfielder, who thrives on crosses for his club. He scored 20 goals for United in 2002-03 including a run of seven in six matches. Yet Eriksson has retained Scholes at the front of his midfield diamond. He said: 'It doesn't concern me that he hasn't scored for a while, because he's still scoring regularly for United.'

Undisputed regular

Scholes has been an undisputed regular for the past five years. Now he faces a challenge from the emerging Frank Lampard – and from Rooney, who played in the 'hole' against Macedonia and Liechtenstein when Scholes was injured.

Scholes is known as the quiet man of Old Trafford. But he can point to an impressive record with United, and with England. Goals flowed in his early appearances. He netted on his England debut against Italy in 1997 and against Tunisia in the 1998 World Cup finals. He became the first England player since Ian Wright to score a hat-trick when he grabbed all three against Poland in Kevin Keegan's debut match as national coach.

FACT FILE

Club: Manchester United
Born: Salford, 16 November 1974
England caps: 59 (57 starts, 2 as sub)
England goals: 13

Best moment for England: Becoming the first England player since Ian Wright to score a hat-trick when he netted all three goals in the 3-1 win against Poland in the Euro 2000 qualifier at Wembley

John Terry

Relishing the Battle

John Terry is an uncomplicated centre-back. He loves to defend. He is the lineal descendant of England stalwarts such as Tony Adams and Terry Butcher, happy to lay their bodies on the line to keep opponents out. Like Adams and Butcher, Terry lacks pace. Like them, he makes up for it with anticipation, aerial power, fierce tackling and physical presence.

Butcher admires Terry, not least for the Chelsea defender's display in England's 0-0 draw against Turkey. He said: 'It was a big character test for Terry and he passed it. You have to admire the discipline he showed.' Terry said: 'It was one of the toughest games I've played in, but it was a great experience. I still think Sol and Rio are Sven's first choice. But I obviously want to play and when I'm called on, I have to do well.'

The right attitude

Terry made a belated England debut in the friendly against Serbia-Montenegro in June 2003. He had been excluded from selection for England because of a court case after an incident at a west London club. He was cleared of assault charges, but the affair made him think about his attitude. He said: 'In the summer [of 2002], I had a chat with a few people about the kind of person I wanted to be. I knew that I had to sort myself out. I've made some mistakes, but I hold my hand up for them. Now I do a lot more work at training. I look after my body and I'm feeling the benefits.'

Terry, Chelsea – and England – are reaping the rewards.

FACT FILE

Club: Chelsea
Born: Bermondsey, 7 December 1980
England caps: 6 (5 starts, 1 as sub)
England goals: 0

Best moment for England: His commanding defensive performance in the 0-0 draw against Turkey in Istanbul which earned him the plaudits and the Man of the Match award

James Beattie
Striker ◆ Age 26

Striking Ambition

James Beattie forced his way into England contention with his scoring feats for Southampton in 2002-03. He finished as the leading English marksman in the Premiership with 23 goals and helped the Saints reach the FA Cup final.

He made his international debut in the friendly against Australia in February 2003 and has become a regular in Sven-Goran Eriksson's squad this season, though he's still seeking his first England goal. He said: 'Once I'd been called up, I wanted more. Getting into the squad is one thing, getting into the team is another. That's my ambition.'

Beattie joined Southampton from Blackburn in 1998 but his career took off after Gordon Strachan arrived as manager.

Peter Reid, who tried to sign the young Beattie for Sunderland, said: 'In his early days at Blackburn, he was a strong raw target man who was good in the air. He has developed tremendously under Gordon at Southampton.'

Former England great Alan Shearer added: 'James has worked so hard on his game. He has the ability to make difficult chances look easy.' Now he must complete the step-up from club to England stardom.

FACT FILE

Club: Southampton
Born: Lancaster, 27 February 1978
England caps: 5 (2 starts, 3 as sub)
England goals: 0
Best moment for England:
Making his debut, against Australia

Wayne Bridge
Defender ◆ Age 23

Keeping Focused

Leicester manager Mickey Adams will never forget his first meeting with Wayne Bridge. Adams was working for Southampton at the time. He said: 'I went to a park match in Winchester one Sunday. I noticed this brilliant little left-winger. I spoke to his parents and the next night he came along to Southampton's academy.' That was Bridge's first step on the road to a senior career. He switched to left-back as he rose through the Saints' ranks. His defensive qualities earned him a full debut in the friendly against Holland.

Southampton boss Gordon Strachan said: 'Wayne's greatest strength is his strength. He works so hard to keep himself fit that his body is ready for anything. He doesn't dive into tackles or get emotional. He just keeps focused.'

Bridge impressed a national audience with displays as Southampton reached the 2003 FA Cup final. His reward was a £7 million summer transfer to Chelsea as Roman Abramovich began to build his super squad.

He is convinced that joining such a high-profile club will boost his England chances. He said: 'I'd like to let Ashley Cole know that I'm on his heels, because I want to play for England.'

FACT FILE

Club: Chelsea
Born: Southampton, 5 August 1980
England caps: 15 (8 starts, 7 as sub)
England goals: 0
Best moment for England:
Making his debut, against Holland

Joe Cole | Midfielder ◆ Age 22

A Diamond Yet to be Polished

Joe Cole remains a case of potential yet to be fulfilled. As a youngster, the ex-West Ham midfielder was hailed as the answer to England's prayers. He played in the opening game of the 2002 World Cup finals against Sweden as a 20-year-old. But he has yet to establish himself in Sven-Goran Eriksson's engine room.

Cole is still trying to establish himself in the Premiership too, following his £6.6 million move to Chelsea. Claudio Ranieri has preferred to use him as an impact player, stepping off the bench, rather than a starter. Eriksson has employed Cole in similar fashion. He has gained 11 of his 12 caps as a sub.

There's no doubting Cole's vision and ball skills. But critics question the end product of his work and worry about his awareness of other players. Eriksson said: 'I said when I first came to England that Cole is one of the greatest talents that you can find. He's a diamond that you have to polish because the tactical side of his game is not his strongest.'

Yet Cole struck England's winner in the friendly against Serbia with a free kick that would have done credit to David Beckham. It was a measure of his talent to be tapped.

FACT FILE

Club: Chelsea
Born: Islington, 8 November 1981
England caps: 13 (2 start, 11 as sub)
England goals: 2
Best moment for England: Playing in the World Cup as a 20-year-old

Kieron Dyer | Midfielder ◆ Age 25

Major Talent

Kieron Dyer is another still to make his mark for England. The Newcastle midfielder has touch, pace and frequently pops up unmarked in the box. He can play wide on the right, in central midfield, or even as a support striker.

Dyer has been handicapped by a series of injuries, most notably the shin splint problem which troubled him throughout the 2001-02 campaign. Sven-Goran Eriksson was desperate to give him a run before the World Cup finals, but knocks kept getting in the way.

The ex-Ipswich midfielder has made most of his England appearances as a sub. Eriksson sees Dyer's speed as a weapon to unleash against a tiring defence, the role that he filled in the closing stages of the 0-0 draw in Turkey. But Dyer had yet to score after 19 caps. His club manager Sir Bobby Robson, the former England chief, believes he must find that cutting edge if he is to force his way into Eriksson's starting team.

Sir Bobby said: 'Kieron is a major talent, but he has to start scoring more goals. He has everything else in his game. He makes these superb runs, he can beat players with skill, then he doesn't finish properly.'

FACT FILE

Club: Newcastle United
Born: Ipswich, 29 December 1978
England caps: 19 (7 starts, 12 as sub)
England goals: 0
Best moment for England: Making his debut, against Luxembourg

Owen Hargreaves
Midfielder • Age 23

Energetic and Versatile

Owen Hargreaves grew up in Canada, plays in Germany, has a Welsh mother – and chose to turn out for his father's country, England. Dad Colin obviously influenced Owen's decision. Hargreaves senior is a big Bolton fan and Owen said: 'If I came to play in England, my dad would love me to play for Bolton.'

Hargreaves joined Bayern as a 16-year-old, on the recommendation of a Calgary-based German coach. He said: 'I was a long way from home and a long way from the first team, but that became my ambition.'

He showed his class in the closing stages of the Champions League in 2001, deputising for suspended playmaker Stefan Effenberg as Bayern beat Real Madrid, then Valencia in the final, to win the European Cup.

Sven-Goran Eriksson gave Hargreaves his full England debut against Holland in August 2001. His energy and versatility have made him an integral member of the squad ever since. Hargreaves has also played right wing-back and midfield anchor for Bayern – and subbed for Danny Mills at right-back in the Euro 2004 qualifier against Slovakia.

FACT FILE

Club: Bayern Munich
Born: Calgary, 20 January 1981
England caps: 15 (6 starts, 9 as sub)
England goals: 0
Best moment for England:
Beating Germany 5-1 in Munich

Paul Robinson
Goalkeeper • Age 24

Facing the Challenge

Paul Robinson made an impression on Sven-Goran Eriksson when he was still in charge at Lazio. Robinson was standing in for the injured Nigel Martyn in the Champions League game in Rome in December 2000. Robinson's performance that night earned him man of the match accolades. Eriksson's assistant that night, Roberto Mancini, said: 'Robinson caught Sven's eye in that game. His handling was brilliant, he read crosses well and he looked very safe with shots.'

Eriksson later described the Leeds keeper as 'one of the big talents coming up'. But Robinson had to wait until the start of the 2002-03 season before displacing Martyn as Leeds' number 1. He played in every game, building his reputation despite Leeds' struggles. He quickly became a transfer target, although a summer move to join former Leeds boss

David O'Leary at Aston Villa, fell through.

Meanwhile, Robinson made his England debut as a sub in the friendly against Australia in February 2003. He has established himself as David James's international understudy, though he may yet face a challenge from another young keeper, Liverpool's Chris Kirkland.

FACT FILE

Club: Leeds United
Born: Beverley, 15 October 1979
England caps: 4 (4 as sub)
Best moment for England:
Making his debut, against Australia

Matthew Upson
Defender • Age 24

Always Improving

Matthew Upson made the break from Arsenal in 2003 – and he's never looked back. The Gunners signed Upson from Luton in the summer of 1997. But he had to join Birmingham to become a first-team regular and break into the England squad. Upson made his England debut as a substitute in the 2-1 friendly win over South Africa. Then he started the home Euro 2004 qualifying wins over Slovakia and Liechtenstein.

Former Gunners' and England skipper Tony Adams always forecast a bright future for Upson. But injuries hindered his progress at Highbury. When he was fit, there were always foreign squad players – Gilles Grimandi, Pascal Cygan, Oleg Luzhny and Igors Stepanovs – ahead of him. Upson said: 'Not many players leave Arsenal and progress, but being with England makes me realise what a good decision I made.

I knew I could do well at the top level.

'Birmingham have provided me with a breath of fresh air. I've settled in quickly and I'm happy.' Birmingham boss Steve Bruce, the former Manchester United centre-back, said: 'Matthew has been so impressive. I think he's the best left-footed centre-back in the country and he'll keep improving'.

FACT FILE

Club: Birmingham City
Born: Eye, Suffolk, 18 April 1979
England caps: 6 (4 starts, 2 as sub)
England goals: 0
Best moment for England: Making his debut, against South Africa

Darius Vassell
Striker • Age 23

There's No Substitute

Darius Vassell scored probably the most important goal in England's Euro 2004 qualifying campaign. But he's still not sure of a place at Aston Villa. Vassell stepped from the bench to stab in a rebound off goalkeeper Rustu Recber, at Sunderland, to set England on the way to a 2-0 win over Turkey in April 2003.

Sven-Goran Eriksson has used Vassell as a tactical weapon or as a deputy for Michael Owen. Most of his England appearances have been as a sub. The Villa striker stepped off the bench in Istanbul to run at tiring defenders, a role that is his forte. He had been called into the squad because of an injury to Owen. Then it was back to Villa, to compete for a place with Colombian striker Juan Pablo Angel and Sweden's Marcus Allback.

Vassell's biggest asset is his speed, as Angel testifies: 'Darius has the pace to frighten any defender in the world.'

Vassell has also gained plenty of international experience since making a spectacular full debut, scoring against Holland in February 2002. He also started against Sweden in the 2002 World Cup finals.

FACT FILE

Club: Aston Villa
Born: Sutton Coldfield, 13 June 1980
England caps: 15 (5 starts, 10 as sub)
England goals: 4
Best moment for England: Scoring on his debut, against Holland

Ian Walker
Goalkeeper ◆ Age 32

Club: Leicester City
Born: Watford, 31 October 1971
England caps: 3

Walker was recalled to the England squad against South Africa in the summer of 2003, six years after winning his last cap. He established himself as Sven-Goran Eriksson's third keeper, without adding to his cap total. He made his three England appearances as a Tottenham player, coming on as a sub against Hungary and China and starting against Italy. He is the son of ex-Watford keeper and Norwich and Everton manager, Mike Walker.

Danny Mills
Defender ◆ Age 26

Club: Middlesbrough (on loan)
Born: Norwich, 18 May 1977
England caps: 18 **England goals:** 0

Mills came to the fore at the 2002 World Cup finals when he deputised for the injured Gary Neville. Critics questioned his disciplinary record, but the former Norwich and Charlton right-back was on his best behaviour in Japan. He was also one of the heroes of England's 1-0 win over Argentina. He has slipped down the pecking order after being substituted three minutes before half-time during the Euro 2004 qualifier against Slovakia in June 2003. He joined Middlesbrough on loan this season after a disagreement with Leeds manager Peter Reid.

Jonathon Woodgate
Defender ◆ Age 24

Club: Newcastle United
Born: Middlesbrough, 22 January 1980
England caps: 4 **England goals** 0

Woodgate is rebuilding his career at Newcastle after he was found guilty of affray in a high-profile court case while he was with Leeds. Though acquitted of a charge of causing grievous bodily harm, he was excluded from selection for the 2002 World Cup squad. Woodgate, who made his England debut against Bulgaria in 1999, was recalled for the friendly against Portugal and played in the early Euro 2004 qualifiers against Slovakia and Macedonia. He was forced to pull out of the squad against Macedonia and Liechtenstein in 2003 because of a stomach muscle problem.

Jermaine Jenas
Midfielder ◆ Age 21

Club: Newcastle United
Born: Nottingham, 18 February 1983
England caps: 4 **England goals:** 0

Newcastle paid £5 million – the second-highest ever fee for a teenager – to sign Jenas from Nottingham Forest in February 2002. The attacking midfielder graduated from England's Under-21s to the first team for the friendly against Australia a year later. He appeared in two more summer friendlies before returning to the Under-21s to tighten his approach. He has won eight Under-21 caps and skippered the side against Turkey in October.

David Dunn
Midfielder ◆ Age 24

Club: Birmingham City
Born: Blackburn, 27 December 1979
England caps: 1 England goals: 0

Dunn made his only England appearance in the September 2002 friendly against Portugal. He says: 'I don't want to be a one-cap wonder. I've had a taste of international football and I want to be knocking on the door again.' His career has gained fresh impetus after a £5.5 million summer move from home town club Blackburn to Birmingham. Dunn had been with Blackburn since leaving school.

Danny Murphy
Midfielder ◆ Age 27

Club: Liverpool
Born: Chester, 18 March 1977
England caps: 9 England goals: 1

Murphy was given his chance by Sven-Goran Eriksson and scored in England's 2002 World Cup warm-up win over Paraguay. He missed the finals after falling awkwardly in training and breaking a toe in his left foot. Murphy played in Liverpool's 2001 FA Cup and UEFA Cup-winning sides. He is tactically astute and something of a free-kick expert. He made his name at Crewe and joined Liverpool for £2 million in the summer of 1997.

Alan Smith
Striker ◆ Age 23

Club: Leeds United
Born: Rothwell, Leeds, 20 October 1980
England caps: 6 England goals: 1

Smith is Leeds through and through. He scored on his debut at Liverpool in November 1998 and has stuck with Leeds despite their recent problems. He had a spell in midfield under Terry Venables but has now returned to a striking role. Smith made his England debut against Mexico as a 20-year-old, in May 2001. He headed England's goal in the 1-1 friendly draw with Portugal when he was named Man of the Match. But he has been out of favour with England since he was sent off for a second yellow card against Macedonia in the Euro 2004 qualifier at Southampton.

Jermain Defoe
Striker ◆ Age 21

Club: West Ham United
Born: Beckton, 7 October 1982
England caps: 0 England goals: 0

Defoe is small, quick and a predator in the box. He is a veteran of England's Under-21 squad – scoring seven times in 20 games – but has yet to step up to full international status. West Ham hung onto him after their relegation, but the £10 million-rated striker is expected to leave unless the Hammers regain their Premiership status. He has already been linked with several major clubs.

SVEN-GORAN ERIKSSON

England Coach ◆ Age 55

Quiet Man Who Rouses Passions

Sven-Goran Eriksson divides fans and media. To many, he is a cerebral coach who has proved himself at the highest level, with Gothenburg, Benfica and Lazio. He turned round England's World Cup qualifying campaign, then steered his squad into Euro 2004 without losing a game. On the way they beat Turkey, who finished third in the 2002 World Cup. Critics say he lacks passion. They point to England's second-half performance against 10-man Brazil in the World Cup quarter-finals – and claim that Eriksson failed to motivate the side. Others question his commitment, in the light of speculation linking him with Chelsea.

Eriksson doesn't pace the touchline, raging with emotion. His expression rarely flickers beyond a smile. He speaks in guarded sentences. He declined to make a public stand on the Rio Ferdinand controversy before the qualifier in Turkey. He will back his judgement with a gamble though. Eriksson decided to start with 17-year-old Wayne Rooney against Turkey at Sunderland – and to keep faith with the Everton

youngster in Istanbul. Eriksson stuck with David James in goal although West Ham were relegated.

Sven delivers

When it comes to results, he has delivered. He has lost only one of 19 competitive matches as England coach and that was to the 2002 World Cup winners. He has led England to automatic qualification for two major tournaments. His squad set a record of eight consecutive international victories. Not even Sir Alf Ramsey's side did that.

Eriksson has laboured under the usual handicaps: frequent clashes with leading Premiership clubs to get his stars released; friendlies made meaningless by a batch of enforced substitutions and inflated expectations stoked by those who lay in wait for England coaches.

He has faced an extra obstacle too. There are those who can never forgive him because he wasn't born English.

But his players believe in him. Steven Gerrard said after the draw in Istanbul: 'It's very important that he takes us into Euro 2004. I don't think there's anyone better.'

David James added: 'Sven is the man who has got us there. His record since taking over for the World Cup qualifiers is fantastic.'

Sven is joined in training by his assistant Tord Grip (left) and Brian Kidd (right).

ERIKSSON'S ENGLAND RECORD IN COMPETITIVE GAMES

[UP TO 31 OCTOBER 2003]

WORLD CUP 2002 QUALIFIERS

Date	Venue	Opponents	Score
24 March 2001	Anfield	Finland	2-1
28 March 2001	Tirana	Albania	3-1
6 June 2001	Athens	Greece	2-0
1 September 2001	Munich	Germany	5-1
5 September 2001	Newcastle	Albania	2-0
6 October 2001	Old Trafford	Greece	2-2

WORLD CUP 2002 FINALS JAPAN-KOREA

2 June	Saitama	Sweden (Group Stage)	1-1
7 June	Sapporo	Argentina (Group Stage)	1-0
12 June	Osaka	Nigeria (Group Stage)	0-0
15 June	Nigata	Denmark (2nd Round)	3-0
21 June	Shizuoka	Brazil (Quarter-final)	1-2

EURO 2004 QUALIFIERS

12 October 2002	Bratislava	Slovakia	2-1
16 October 2002	Southampton	Macedonia	2-2
29 March 2003	Vaduz	Liechtenstein	2-0
1 April 2003	Sunderland	Turkey	2-0
11 June 2003	Middlesbrough	Slovakia	2-1
6 September 2003	Skopje	Macedonia	2-1
10 September 2003	Old Trafford	Liechtenstein	2-0
11 October 2003	Istanbul	Turkey	0-0

RECORD

P	W	D	L	F	A
19	13	5	1	36	13

CREDITS

Editor: Julian Flanders
Picture Researcher: Jen Little
Designer: Carole McDonald

NOTE
Players' cap and goal statistics are correct up to 31 December 2003

Come On England!